Moving Forward

RABHYA RAJ SINGH

INDIA • SINGAPORE • MALAYSIA

ISBN
Hardcase 979-8-89588-950-3
Paperback 979-8-89588-332-7

Contents

Foreword

Losing a parent is one of the hardest challenges anyone can face, and for teenagers, this experience can feel uniquely overwhelming, especially when cultural expectations, family dynamics, and personal identity are intertwined with grief. For many, the loss of a parent happens later in life, after years of shared memories and guidance. But when this loss comes during the pivotal teenage years, it can leave a young person navigating not only sorrow and confusion but also the cultural nuances of how grief is understood and expressed.

In Moving Forward, Rabhya Raj Singh shares her personal journey of losing her father, weaving her story with insights and reflections that resonate deeply with those who have experienced loss at a young age. Through the lens of her multicultural background, Rabhya explores the emotions that come with grief—confusion, sadness, anger, and even moments of unexpected joy. These emotions are deeply human, but how we process them can be shaped by the traditions and values we grow up with. Rabhya's journey shows that grief is not something to be rushed through or solved, but a process to be experienced fully, even when it feels chaotic.

This book offers readers a safe space to reflect on their own experiences with grief, drawing on activities and journaling prompts that encourage self-expression. Whether through writing, art, or quiet reflection, these creative outlets provide a powerful means for processing emotions in a way that feels authentic. For Rabhya, rituals like journaling and holding onto personal mementos allowed her to stay connected to her father's memory, while also honoring the cultural practices of her family. In the same way, this book encourages readers to explore their own ways of remembering and honoring their loved one, whether through cultural traditions, family customs, or personal rituals.

Moving Forward also embraces the idea that grief, especially in cultures like those of India and Ghana, is not just an individual experience but one that is shared with family, community, and even ancestors. Funerals, memorials, and spiritual practices often provide a framework for expressing loss, offering both structure and comfort. Rabhya's experience highlights the importance of these cultural practices, from the vibrant funerals in Ghana to the deep spiritual rituals of Hinduism. This book encourages readers to lean into their own traditions, using them to process their emotions, connect with their heritage, and find meaning in loss.

Throughout the book, there are gentle reminders that it's okay to seek support from loved ones, friends, or professionals. Grief can feel isolating, but it can also be a collective experience; one that communities can help to carry. Whether it's through the love of family, the support of friends, or the wisdom of cultural practices, this book reminds readers that they don't have to navigate their grief alone.

Moving Forward is more than just a guide for healing; it's a companion for readers who are navigating the emotional and cultural complexities of grief. Rabhya's story, filled with personal reflections and cultural insights, shows that while grief may change our lives, it doesn't have to define them. By holding onto the memories of those we've lost, and by honoring them in ways that are meaningful, we can find our way through the hardest moments. Grief may be a long journey, but with time, support, and love, readers will discover that it's possible to smile again, to find joy, and to create new memories while still cherishing the past.

Kongit Farrell, M.A., M.S., L.M.F.T

Kongit Farrell

Kongit is a licensed Marriage, Family and Couples therapist (CA-97773), AASECT-certified Sex Therapist, Trauma-trained therapist, and Conflict Resolution Expert. Her therapeutic approach is evidence-based and firmly rooted in CBT, Developmental, and Solution-Focused methodologies. She is an Adjunct Professor of Clinical Psychology at Pepperdine University, Clinical Supervisor for associate marriage and family therapists, counselors, and social workers and is the Founder of the Inspired Journey Counseling Center in Downtown Los Angeles. As a peacebuilder, she sits on YPO's executive board for the Global Peace Network.

She has received advanced training in Cognitive Behavioral Therapy from The Beck Institute for Cognitive Behavioral Therapy, Couples Therapy from The Gottman Institute, Sexuality from the Center for Healthy Sex in Los Angeles, and The Buehler Institute in Orange County. She received training and education at the UN's University for Peace in Costa Rica in Positive Leadership and has presented at their Gross Global Happiness Summit. She is trained in Global Mental Health and Trauma Recovery (for refugees and victims of trauma) by Harvard Medical School.

Kongit's work and research in Peacebuilding is focused on helping to establish harmony in couples and families. She is a former AC4 and CMM Fellow, both from Columbia University in NYC, where she earned her second master's degree in Conflict Resolution with an emphasis in Mediation.

As a leader in her field, Kongit was elected as the Membership Chair of the California Association of Marriage & Family Therapists in Los Angeles for a 2-year term.

The death of a parent is an incalculable loss
because no one will ever love you like that again

Chapter One

Have you ever been caught in a whirlwind of emotions? Something huge in your life changed, making your world turn upside down? Well, you're not alone. Life has its own way of throwing unexpected challenges our way, and one of the toughest can be losing someone we love.

28.06.22; 12:00 Noon; Accra, Ghana

Light illuminated our home as the afternoon sun beamed from corner to corner. My family reciprocated the same energy as today was my older brother, Rudra's high school graduation. An important milestone for him and everyone. Joy echoed around our house as Rudra was chosen by his classmates to deliver the keynote speech. My mum, dad, and I were preparing for the day we had been anticipating. Mum faced a battle between which of her saris she should wear; I was more troubled about my hair and wanted it to look perfect for a perfect day; dad, a fitness enthusiast, who had just come back from the gym wanted his muscles to ripple under the white linen kurta that he planned to wear.

My brother had received his gown and cap. Sneakily, my dad and I tried it and took pictures of it. Rudra hurried down to fetch his gown and saw us clicking pictures. Frustration was evident on his face, as he snatched it back and raced towards the stairs. We giggled and shouted at him, promising to iron it.

We surrounded the dining table for brunch, our conversation obviously revolved around the topic of the day—graduation. As we had a lazy brunch over constant banter, a faint ring came from my dad's pocket. He stepped into another room with his phone in his hand to take the call. As soon as my plate became empty, I rushed up to my room, deciding to face the challenge of what should I wear. Whilst I was caught up in doing my hair and picking my shoes, the downstairs of our home had erupted into chaos. In oblivion, I continued what I was doing until my phone echoed a desperate ring from my brother.

"Rabhya, papa is gone."

Confusion riddled my mind and all forms of thought and movement evacuated from my body. My dad suffered a heart attack, and I did not even realize it. I thought today would be the perfect day, nothing could go wrong, nothing was supposed to go wrong! What did he mean? Where had Papa gone on graduation day? Where could he go? In a fraction of a second, my world collapsed. My father wasn't there and my mother wasn't acting like herself. With the small courage I had left, I descended downstairs. Our house was swarming with people. Everyone gave me that look of compassion. Some hugged me while some asked me to be strong. But all I could focus on was my mother. I scanned the room attempting to spot my mother out of the hundreds of people. There she was, surrounded by people, looking stunned.

"Mama," I whispered. No response. I whispered again, "Mama?" but she didn't respond. I sat in a quiet corner of my house. What just happened? How could he leave me? How could he leave us? I thought that everything that was going on belonged in my nightmare, that I would wake up and it would all be different.

Instead, the next morning I was greeted by even more uncertainty than the day before.

My father was gone and my mother became a mere shadow of her feisty self.

The emotions I was confronted with were unfamiliar to me. I couldn't breathe, my hands trembled, and I was angry. I was infuriated at my father but I believed that he would come back, like he always did. While everyone asked me to be strong, I wondered "Strong for what?" I wanted to scream. I needed my father. This wasn't real. This wasn't happening to me.

"Grief" became a word I suddenly had frequent encounters with. This unfamiliar word was used to describe what my family and I were going through. I soon learned that it's a word that describes the mix of emotions we feel when we lose someone or something important. It is a bit of a complex journey with multiple pitstops, detours, and halts.

The thing is, it's okay to feel all sorts of things along this emotional journey. But how do we cope with it?

The Stages of Grief

Think of grief as a path with different pit stops—each representing a unique feeling you might experience. Grief can be understood and manifested in many different ways. In general, these help one understand what they're feeling. Let's dive deeper into these steps:

Denial

This is the first stop on our journey. Denial is like saying, "No, this can't be happening!" It's a natural reaction as big changes can be difficult to accept. Your mind needs time to catch up with what's going on around you.

Anger

You might feel a surge of frustration or even anger towards the world or the person who left. It's equivalent to having a bundle of accreted energy inside you, and it's perfectly okay to let those emotions out. Anger is just another part of the journey.

Bargaining

Making deals with the universe, we might often think, "If only *I* did things differently, maybe everything would change." It's a natural part of trying to make sense of things, even if the outcome is beyond our control.

Depression

At this stop, one feels really sad and lonely. It's okay to cry and express these emotions. It might feel like you're in a dark tunnel, but remember, there's always a way out, even if it takes time.

Acceptance

This is the end of the rollercoaster ride. It doesn't mean you forget the person or the way things were, but you start finding new ways to live without them. It's a bit like learning to dance to a new song.

My life was inflicted with changes out of my control, changes that I disliked. I needed to find a way to channel my emotions by better understanding it. One way that greatly helped me was writing things down in a diary.

<u>JOURNAL:</u>

Imagine these feelings as different friends visiting you during tough times. First, there's Denial, the friend who says, "No way, this can't be happening!" Then, Anger shows up, helping you release frustration like a mini firework show in your heart. Bargaining is like making a deal to fix things, and Depression is the friend who makes you feel really, really sad on those tough days. Finally, there's Acceptance, a friend helping you find a new way to live, like learning a cool dance move to a different tune. Write about when each friend visited you, how they made you feel, and how your understanding of them has changed since the start of your journey. It's like telling a story about your feelings growing and changing!

Grief is a Strange Companion

Now, here's something important to understand about grief—it's not a linear path as most people suggest. No one will go through these stages in the same order, and sometimes, just like me, you might find yourself revisiting one stage multiple times. Grief is unpredictable and it's okay if it feels messy. It's normal to go back and forth between these feelings, and not rush through them.

You might wake up one-day feeling a sense of acceptance and the next day, anger might sneak in. And that's okay too. Grief is a personal journey, and everyone experiences it differently. Like a box of crayons, you might use different colors to paint your emotions each day.

<u>JOURNAL:</u>

Imagine your feelings as if they were on a rollercoaster ride! Get colorful markers and picture a squiggly, twisty line going up and down like the craziest roller coaster you've ever seen. Mark the high points as "Peaks" and the not-so-high moments as "Dips." Now, give each of these points a name like "Happiness" or "Confusion," relating to how you might have felt in a high point and the not so high point. Use your most exciting colors to show how strong each feeling is—think bright red for super excitement and cool blue for when things are a bit calm. This emotional rollercoaster is all yours, and by drawing it, you get to understand the twists and turns of your feelings!

The Heart aches In Different Ways

Everyone's healing process is personal to them. Everyone has different ways of dealing with challenges that they are faced with. Here are a few ways we might express our feelings during the journey of grief.

Questioning

A lot of questions brew in our minds. The brain asks why things happen or what comes next. It's a way of trying to make sense of the world around us.

Artistic Expression

Sometimes suppressed feelings flow through art, writing, or theater. Drawing pictures or writing stories are like little messages to internal feelings.

The Tortoise

Then, there is the quiet thinking. We withdraw in our shells and do not say much, but that doesn't mean we're not feeling. A lot is happening inside. Sometimes, we need a bit of extra time and space.

The Helper

Sometimes we like to help others as a way of coping. It could be taking care of a pet or helping our loved ones with chores. Helping can give us a sense of control in a world that might feel a bit unpredictable.

Chapter Two

Grief is a heavy word, much like a cloud that hangs over everything. For me, it means feeling sad because something important and special has changed or is missing. I constantly felt this deep sadness because my father, who I love the most in this world, was gone. In this chapter, we are going to talk about how to understand what's happening inside of ourselves.

Crack The Code To Your Body's Messages

I had stopped going out to play and I just wanted to stay inside my bathroom biting my nails or staring at the lone lizard on the wall. I stopped eating on the dining table, instead I brought my food in my room and did not eat at all. How could I eat? My father wasn't there and I rejected everything that was nourishing. I gagged just looking at the plate of food. I needed my father and not a plate of food.

And **YOU?**

When you are going through this journey, you'll feel many different emotions that might be hard to understand. Sometimes, when we're feeling sad, we don't know how to explain it. Our heart is carrying a big weight and we're not sure how to share it with others. Sometimes we feel tired and don't want to play or do things like we used to. Some people might cry a lot or get mad easily. Others might have tummy aches, headaches, or experience more physical changes.

I sometimes would get really annoyed, then sad, then extremely happy, then tired, or I would start feeling sick. You might also have a hard time paying attention in class or doing things you usually enjoy. Look out for changes in how you behave, feel, and think. I started to realize that sometimes I didn't want to do things like play sports which I used to find joy in, maybe because they reminded me of what I used to do with my dad or maybe because there was so much going on in my life, I lost the spark of what I once loved to do. I wasn't myself anymore.

Becoming Detectives of Our Behavior

My world seemed different now. Key parts of my life had been removed.

And for you, you might not want to play games or go outside. Maybe you're quieter or get annoyed more easily. It's okay if you're not the same right now. Grief does that to us, it changes things. It still happens to me. Grief can make you feel a bit confused and maybe forgetful, like forgetting where you put your toys or books. All the feelings are mixed up, and that's completely fine. People might ask you how you are doing, it shows that they care. Something you have to learn is that it's okay to tell them how you feel, it's okay to share some of the burden that is upon you.

I realized that I would start getting annoyed more easily, little things would bother me. The journey through grief impacts us in so many ways, and through this process the way we view or deal with things may change.

Sailing the Sea of Feelings

The feelings that I am sailing through is a big tangled jumble. Sometimes, sad, angry, confused, annoyed, tired, scared and sometimes experience it all in full totality. Constantly riding a rollercoaster of emotions, and not sure when it's going to stop.

And **YOU**...

Crying is okay, it helps me let out what I am feeling even when I do not feel like talking. It's not a sign of weakness—it's your heart letting out some of that heavy sadness. Your friends might not understand everything, but they want to help. If you want to talk, they'll listen. If you want to be alone, they'll understand that too.

I realized that it is important to find a space to let out what you are feeling instead of bottling it up. In some ways, if you do not confront them, they find other ways of creeping up. I started to fall sick easily, and after a few visits to the doctor, we realized that these are the emotions that I have been bottling up. If you do not deal with the emotions you are confronted with, they will find other ways to explode.

Exploring the Land of Thought

Brain fog and more brain fog; I couldn't think straight or focus in class anymore. I was wallowing in grief. I was imagining various situations like how my father pranked us and suddenly he was back. Sometimes it was an unknown fear of the future. This affected my cognitive abilities in school and outside. I felt trapped between nostalgia and remorse.

Imagine your brain as a chaotic room and each of your thoughts and emotions being scattered everywhere. Because of this, it might be hard to concentrate on certain things, maybe it is in school, and it is because there is so much you need to process that your mind might stray away.

If you're struggling with schoolwork or forgetting things, it's okay to ask for help. Something that I did was communicating to my friends when I was finding it difficult to concentrate on certain subjects and if they could just sit with me and explain concepts to me. You can do the same, create your own circle or tutors who can help you if you are struggling with academics.

Understanding Feelings at Every Age

I was confused. I didn't know how to behave, respond or feel. I sometimes pretended to be happy and cool even though I felt miserable inside. Attending social gatherings was the hardest part as I just didn't understand how to reciprocate the love, compassion and care that came my way.

It all really depends on one's age for a large part. Your reaction will be different. If you are around 5-8 years olds, it's hard to understand what's happening. That's why you get clingy or act out. That's okay; you're just trying to make sense of this big change.

If you're in middle childhood, like 9-12 years old, you might understand your emotions a bit more, but you might also try to hide your feelings. It's okay to show them—it doesn't make you weak. People will understand and empathize with you because everyone feels sad sometimes.

As a teenager, you might want to handle things on your own. I always thought that I would not want to burden anyone else with what I was going through, or I wanted to act as if nothing happened because sometimes it is just easier that way. I learned that it is important to talk about your feelings. If I missed my dad, I learned to express myself. Even though people thought that it would make you feel sad, it would actually help relieve the tension you felt in the moment, and maybe you can find a way to create new memories with your loved one.

As you navigate the sea of complex emotions, it is important to have something that guides you like a sailor. Let this journal be like that for you, how my diary was for me.

<u>JOURNAL:</u>

Imagine this page is the sky and draw a big cloud. Picture this cloud as a magical mix of colors, like a rainbow of feelings. When you feel sad because of grief, you can use your crayons to color the cloud. Maybe blue for the sad moments, red for the times you get a bit mad, and other colors for different emotions. This colorful cloud is your own emotions party, showing you all the feelings you have inside. It's a way to have an image of all the emotions you are feeling.

Chapter Three

Imagine communication strategies as special tools we use to talk and listen for the best outcome possible. It's like a secret code that is personal to us that helps us share our thoughts and feelings in the way we understand them the best. In this chapter, we'll learn how to use age-appropriate language, create a safe space for talking, tackle tricky questions, and straighten out common misconceptions.

What Is Your Communication Language?

How do you prefer to communicate? What is your love language? Do you find a quiet corner and talk to yourself? For me, I find solace in writing my emotions because I am able to clear my head, write down what I am feeling, release it from myself, and process it. Other ways that I was able to clear my head was by playing the piano or listening to music that might resonate with how I am feeling. But it took me some time to get there.

It's vital to understand that your emotions need to be processed and you need to communicate how you are feeling. Find your language, what makes your head clearer?

Ways that you can communicate your emotions:

<u>Verbal Expression:</u>

Some people enjoy expressing their feelings through words. Example: "I miss playing games with Grandpa. Can we talk about him?"

<u>Artistic Expression:</u>

Another form of communication can be through art. Whether it's drawing, painting or creating crafts, these all hold stories of what you are feeling when voicing them can be difficult. Example: Painting a picture using colors that relate to your emotions.

<u>Play and Imaginative Expression:</u>

Younger children may use play and acting to express their emotions, acting out scenes or using toys to represent their feelings. Example: Playing with dolls or action figures to create scenarios relating to what they are feeling, maybe talking to the loved one or having a pretend conversation about them.

During the grieving process, finding your communication language is important. You need to create a space where you feel safe enough to unpack your feelings in a way that you feel most comfortable with.

<u>JOURNAL:</u>

Think about things that help you clear your head when you are stressed or overwhelmed. Write them down and how they help you. These can be like your communication languages to look back on for when you are feeling overwhelmed and your emotions are all over the place.

Chapter Four

How does one support oneself and their family while wading through the currents of grief? Do you practice self-care first or step-up to fill the shoes of others? Perhaps thinking of the people around you as a team of superheroes, each with their superpowers, who are there to help each other out can be one useful solution.

Family Dynamics

Family dynamics, like the intricate dance of superheroes in a team, play a crucial role in navigating grief. It can influence how individuals within the family experience and cope with loss. These dynamics can impact emotions, communication, and the overall well-being of family members. Creating a supportive grieving environment within the family involves acknowledging individual needs, fostering open communication, and providing mutual support.

Impact on Communication:

My Challenges: Grief can lead to miscommunication. Sometimes I felt that I did not want to share what I am going through, or my brother did not want to share what he is going through.

Positive Approach: We were able to encourage open communication and create a safe space where my mom, brother, and I felt open enough to talk about our struggles with grief.

Individual Coping Styles:

Challenge: Different family members may have unique ways of coping with grief. I felt that I might have kept my grief to myself, my brother's grief resulted in a lack of sleep, anger, and not celebrating things that we normally would have, my mom's grief was different from ours. Suddenly she had unprecedented responsibilities, she never had to deal with bills, bank work, or any form of paper or legal work. And suddenly, she was bombarded with all of these things. It was difficult to understand everyone's emotions and sometimes you might not like how the other person is acting.

Positive Approach: Respect and validate each individual's coping style. Understanding that everyone grieves differently fosters empathy within the family. We continued communicating our struggles. My mom was very open and honest about whatever was going on, through open and honest communication my brother and I were always in the loop and we were able to slowly understand how each of us copes with challenges.

Role Changes:

Challenge: Grief can bring about role changes within the family, affecting responsibilities and expectations. With my father gone, there was a void that we all felt. It was difficult to cope with the fact that the "head of the family" was gone. An important person in our lives was not there anymore and it caused small arguments within the family. We started saying "If Papa was here" in all our arguments.

Positive Approach: Time plays an important factor in this. It takes time, but you will embrace change and be flexible.

<u>*Sibling Relationships:*</u>

Challenge: With my brother and I, at first we did not understand that we grieved differently and maybe the way I coped made him upset or the way he coped made me upset but with open communication, we spoke and found ways to support each other. My mother stayed out of this and she let both of us handle this between us. This brought my brother and I emotionally closer despite the physical distance

Positive Approach: We found things to do with each other like going on drives, or getting ice cream, and fostering a space for communication. And we learned to be more understanding with each other.

<u>JOURNAL:</u>

#1 Imagine you and your siblings as awesome superheroes in a comic strip adventure! Draw frames showing different moments where you support each other. Add speech bubbles to write down what you would say to help each other. It can help understand certain situations and how to empathize and understand each other better.

#2 Write a letter to your older sibling to show them you care and understand if they're feeling sad. Share your feelings and let them know you're there for them. This activity helps you practice expressing your emotions through writing and reminds you of your role as a supportive sibling.

The Role of Schools and Communities

Imagine schools and communities as superheroes joining your team during tough times. They become special friends with powers to help you and your family when you're feeling sad and going through a lot.

I found a lot of support in my school, being where I spent most of my time. Counselors, teachers, and faculty offered me emotional support and provided a safe space for me to express my feelings and concerns. Through my school's emotional counselor, I gained a better understanding of what grief is, its associated processes, and an understanding my emotions. The community was extremely supportive towards me and my family by always checking in, sending food, coordinating visitor timings during condolences, and taking us out for outings. A family that was close to mine even took me on a holiday to Dubai. Our community has been extremely supportive and understanding towards my family and me.

Friends and Peers

Your friends and peers are like superhero buddies during tough times—they can help when you're feeling sad. They understand and care about how you feel, striving to make you feel better. To allow their superhero help to take effect, you can talk to them about what you need and let them be part of your support team.

My friends found ways to help and be there for me even though I did not verbally communicate my emotions to them all the time. For my 14th birthday—the first birthday I had without my dad—my friends planned a surprise birthday party for me. They coordinated with my mum and brought food, played music, and made arrangements for everyone to come to my house. Meanwhile, one of my friends took me out for an ice cream and when I returned home everyone was there.

Through important moments, it feels good to have your friends beside you. On the night before the one-year mark of my dad's passing, my friends came to my house and brought me my favorite ice cream because they understood that I might not have wanted so many people around me. They showed me that they were there for me and that they care.

Navigating grief is never easy, but having friends and peers by your side can make the distance easy to traverse. Friends lend their ears and extend a non-judgmental space where you can freely express your feelings, while peers who have experienced similar losses offer understanding and empathy. Friends play a vital role by providing emotional support, validating your feelings, and acknowledging the challenges you face. Whether it's through comforting words, inclusive activities, or simply being there to hold your hand, their actions forge a sense of connection and belonging during difficult times. Together, they form a support system that guides you through the ups and downs of grief by offerining solace, companionship, and shared experiences as you navigate grief together.

JOURNAL:

Imagine drawing your very own superhero team in your journal – your Support Tree! Grab your brightest markers and start creating this fantastic tree. Draw roots, a sturdy trunk, branches, and leaves, envisioning it as a foundation to build the coolest treehouse ever. Write the names of special people or things on each part that support you during tough times – maybe it's your best friend or a favorite hobby. Add vibrant colors to make your Support Tree burst with life, like rainbow leaves and a solid brown trunk. This drawing is a visual celebration of the amazing support in your life, your superhero squad offering comfort and cheers. It's a fun way to recognize and appreciate the fantastic support around you!

Chapter Five

While grieving, there are so many uncertain things in your life that lack clarity you may see a heap of mess wherever you look. It is important to find something that healthily brings you comfort and helps you clear your head. For me, music and art helped me. I listened to upbeat songs and was able to concentrate on art. Somedays, I drew pictures, doodled art, or even tried my hand at painting. Creative outlets allow us to express ourselves and clear up mental space to think and reflect. The following are some suggestive routes through which you can acquire mental clarity:

Art Therapy

Art therapy is like a colorful adventure where you get to draw and paint your feelings. It's like telling a story without words! You can use crayons, paint, or even make sculptures to show how you feel inside. Creating art helps you understand and deal emotions after losing someone special. It's like turning your feelings into a masterpiece!

Play Therapy

Instead of just playing, you can use toys and games to act out your feelings. It's a bit like telling a story using toys. This special playtime helps you express what's on your mind without talking too much.

Music and Movement

Imagine your favorite song that makes you feel so happy as if you were walking on clouds and rainbows. Well, music and dancing can also help you when you're sad. You can play instruments, dance around, or even sing your heart out. It's like creating a happy rhythm that helps you feel better.

JOURNAL:

Write down songs that make you feel happy, maybe a bit sad, or even super excited! Write about each song and how it makes you feel. Is there a song that feels like a warm hug or one that makes you want to jump around? Share why you love each song and let the music tell your emotions' story!

Chapter Six

In this chapter, we will discuss how to preserve our precious memories with someone who we are unable to create new memories with. It is kind of like having a scrapbook of memories that you can hold onto forever. By having a repository of memories that you can revisit, it becomes easier to allay feelings of loneliness and find a memorabilia to cherish the lost person.

Memory as a Fragrance

I was walking around in Dubai Mall with my family friends. It was a difficult moment. It was here that my Father took me to the ice skating rink while my mother shopped. It was right in this mall, my father bought me my first watch. I couldn't control my emotions. I was angry and sad at the same time. It felt as if I was on cue and all I could smell was the strong oud, a fragrance I identify with my father. He doused liberal amounts of oud on himself and it announced his visit even before he physically entered any space. I started walking faster and my eyes were looking for him. If there is fragrant oud, my father cannot be far behind. He is around. My brain asked me to calm down and sit somewhere but my palpitating heart forced me to look for my father. The heady fragrance of oud and my accelerated heartbeat forced me to run out towards the Dubai fountain. I had tears roling down my cheeks. At that moment I didn't care about the look of disapproval from strangers. I had to trace the smell of my dad. I was exploding into million little shards and I could as well have had a heart attack and died then and there.

Time heals. Now, I use the perfume as a reassurance. I dab a little bit of dad on my wrist and I know he is around. I also spray a little bit of the perfume on my pillow and sleep. I sleep wearing his shirt. Sometimes, I open his cupboard and inhale him and I feel enveloped by his love through the clothes he left with me. My dad always stuck little to-do lists and life maps on doors and mirrors. Now they are our guidelines.

My family wears oud perfume to honor papa and we have found courage to share his clothes with people he truly loved and cared for.

Creating Meaningful Rituals

Imagine creating a secret handshake or a special dance routine that reminds you of someone you love and doing it on a special occasion or a special time. That's like having your very own ritual! Rituals are meaningful traditions that help us remember happy times with our loved ones. You can light a candle on their birthday that you know is for them or make a special meal they love once a week. These little rituals are like tiny hugs that keep the memory of your loved one alive and close to your heart.

How to Create Meaningful Rituals

Light a Candle

Pick a special candle and light it on important days or just when you miss them.

Special Meal

Cook or eat a meal that they loved. It's like sharing a dinner table with memories.

Memory Jar

In a jar, write memories or things you love about this person, whenever you miss them you can read these notes and feel their presence.

Balloon Release

On special occasions, you can get a bunch of helium balloons and write messages or draw pictures reminding you of them and release it.

Star Gazing

Some nights, you can talk to the stars, pick one that stands out to you the most and share stories or simply look around at the beautiful sky.

Playlists

Create a playlist with songs that remind you of this person, and when you miss them just play these songs.

Garden

You can create a garden with your and their favorite plants and take care of it in honor of them.

JOURNAL:

1. *Think about the fun things or special traditions you used to do with your loved one. Write about them, the good times and how they made you feel. After writing, draw pictures or symbols that show what these traditions looked like. Maybe it's a special handshake or a favorite game you played together. Let your drawings bring back those happy memories.*

2. *Create a brand new tradition to remember your loved one. Think about something you can do on special days. Write down your ideas for this new tradition. What will you do, and why is it special? After writing, draw a picture of your new tradition. Use colors and shapes that make you feel good. Let your drawing show why this new tradition is important and makes you happy.*

Memories With Loved Ones

Now, let's talk about making memorials. Memorials are like creating a treasure chest of memories. You can make a scrapbook with pictures, write letters to your loved one, or even plant a tree in their memory. These memorials are like love notes that you can keep forever. You can also make a special spot at home or in the garden where you can go to think about them. It's like having a cozy space full of love and memories.

How to Memorialize Loved Ones

Scrapbook

Collect pictures and make a scrapbook of fun times. It's like creating a storybook of your memories.

Write Letters

Write letters to your loved one, telling them about your day or sharing secrets. It's like sending messages to the stars.

Dedications

You could dedicate a bench or a plaque in honor of the person in a meaningful location and it can be a lasting tribute, a way for everyone to remember them for a very long time.

Scholarships or Funds

You could establish a scholarship or fund in their name which supports a cause they cared about, leaving a lasting legacy.

Keepsakes

Wearing a piece of jewelry or clothing which has reminders of your loved one could be a way to carry their memory with you.

<u>JOURNAL:</u>

Gather some pictures, small items (like a piece of jewelry or a ticket stub), and any notes or letters from or about your loved one. These are like treasures that remind you of happy times. This is a special page for your Memory Collage. Stick these treasures on the page and arrange them in a way that feels right to you. Add captions or write short memories beside each item. Your collage will be a beautiful collection of memories that you can look back on whenever you want.

Pretend you're writing a letter to your loved one who's not with you right now. In this letter, share your feelings, thoughts, and updates about your life. Tell them about your day, your achievements, and the things that made you smile. It's like having a conversation with them. Your letter will be like a message sent straight to their heart.

Celebrating Milestones and Anniversaries

It was my father's 50th birthday and we saw the grace of god. My mother, like a true hero, organized a havan (prayer ceremony) in the morning. We prayed and offered gratitude to Lord Shiva. My father was an ardent Shiva devotee. We made donations and served food in different orphanages, just like he would have wanted. In the evening we wore our finest clothes and hosted the most amazing party to celebrate the Bon vivant, my father. We invited our closest friends and shared food, music and drinks. His friends cut the birthday cake and we shared happy stories. Our house came alive with joyous celebration. My mother, brother, and I hugged each other and looked at the sky. We felt papa smiling.

Imagine having a big celebration for your birthday, right? Well, celebrating milestones and anniversaries of your loved can be as happy as that! It's like throwing a party to remember all the amazing things they did. You can make a special cake or do something they loved to commemorate their birthday. Similar to friendship anniversaries, the anniversary of someone you lost is an occasion to remember them with kindness. These festivities are like confetti sprinkled over their memories, giving them an added touch of magic!

Ways to Celebrate Milestones and Anniversaries

Sharing Stories

On special occasions, you can share your favorite stories with your loved one.

Visiting

If there is a way to visit their resting place, on special occasions, go to where they are buried or where their ashes were scattered.

You could bring flowers and a letter, and spend some time there.

Volunteer

Give back to a community your loved one cared about, volunteer on special dates turning that day into a day of kindness and giving back in honor of them.

Event

Organize a memorial event or gathering. Invite close friends and family to share the special day in honor of your loved one.

<u>JOURNAL:</u>

Imagine there's a special day coming up, like a birthday or an anniversary of something important. Close your eyes and think about how you'd like to celebrate and remember your loved one on that day. Now, instead of writing it down, use your crayons, markers, or colored pencils to draw your celebration ideas. Draw the decorations, the yummy food, and the smiles on everyone's faces. Make it as colorful and happy as you want. Your drawing will be like a plan for a super special celebration in honor of your loved one!

Chapter Seven

When times are hard, developing resilience becomes crucial. It is like having a superhero costume for your emotions; it enables you to get back up. Creating a support network, promoting healthy grief outlets, and developing coping skills are some steps that can help one cultivate resilience.

Creating Coping Skills

"Rabhya will carry the Lincoln Flag in her senior year."

This was a constant refrain I used to hear and secretly looked forward to having it come to action. According to tradition, it is the oldest student who carries the school flag during the parade of nations on International day. I joined Lincoln Community School, Accra Ghana in pre-kindergarten and I must have been the oldest student. I knew this would make my father proud. As I entered the High School, I became more involved in community service just like my father. I ran for student council treasurer and won the election by a huge margin. I couldn't wait to come home and share the news with my mother.

I dashed home right after school with all my friends clapping and cheering for me. I informed my mother and she hugged me tight and said "Champion, Rabhyaaaaaaaa" just like my father would have said.

I have something to tell you, said my mother in a very somber tone.

"We are moving to India."

"You are joking, right?"

I couldn't believe my ears. She said she wanted to inform me first before sending an email to school. I kicked the door and ran to my room. I cried myself to sleep. No no no ... this cannot happen. Accra is my home... my life is here. Lincoln Community School is my playground... I just won my first Student Council Election. Everyone knew I would be President of the Student council during my final year. How can my mom be so cruel? I hate you. I wish my father was here. He would know what to do... our magician. I called my brother to inform him. He was livid on the other side of the Atlantic. My mom had already informed him. Our friends couldn't accept our imminent departure. Suddenly our life was being packed in small and big cardboard boxes and labeled. This house was supposed to host my graduation party. This house that my parents had so lovingly nurtured was a party house for all the uncles and aunties. Our house was the hangout place for everyone. We had to go... I wasn't ready. I will not leave Accra. I was angry and sad. I cried and just couldn't eat. It felt as though someone had punched me in the gut. My father is gone and now my mother was taking away my life—house, friends, school, and the city. I don't want this life... I didn't sign up for this. Where is my father? I want him to come back and make everything back to normal. I want my life back. The packers continued to pack. My brother, who was back from his university, refused to leave Ghana.

How did I cope?

I couldn't cope with this. I'm 14 years old and I have to leave my entire being behind and move to another country. I am still angry with my mom for taking me away from my home, friends and school.

Imagine having a toolbox filled with fantastic instruments that help you handle big emotions. Coping skills are like those tools! It's all about finding what works best for you when you're feeling sad or confused. Maybe it's drawing your feelings, taking deep breaths, or going for a walk. We're all unique, so let's discover your special coping skills that make you feel strong and brave!

Discovering your superhero coping skills is like going on an exciting treasure hunt for tools that make you feel strong and brave. It's all about finding what clicks with you and helps when things may be a little overwhelming. First of all, what does coping mean? To cope is to deal with and try to overcome some difficult situations. How you decide to deal with and overcome difficult situations should be healthy.

When there was so much going on in my life from losing my dad and a year later, moving from the country I have lived in almost my whole life, I felt overwhelmed. Packing up memories from my childhood— memories with my dad, my house, my school, my friends, my whole life—was something I had never anticipated before. I found it difficult to cope with such an unexpected change which I was not on board with. However, I used my communication language of writing to help me understand what I was feeling. I practiced coping skills by setting aside time each day to do things that made me happy, such as baking, or watching something from my childhood.

A way you could find out what works best for you is to ask yourself, "What makes me feel better when things are not okay?" It could be different for everyone, so try a few things to see what fits you best.

<u>JOURNAL:</u>

When things get a little bit difficult and instead of using your given superpowers, you need an extra toolkit to help you, what do you do? What makes you feel better when things are not okay? List these things out and draw symbols to represent each of them.

Knowing if these tools are healthy is a skill too. You should check if they make you feel better in a positive way. Do they bring a sense of calm or clarity? If yes, then they're like a magical wand that works wonders. And if you notice they're not helping or making things worse, it's time to explore new tools in your toolbox.

<u>JOURNAL:</u>

Using the list of things that you think help you feel better even when things are not going so well, draw each of their symbols and write a caption on how they help you, this will help you determine if this coping strategy in your toolbox is healthy or unhealthy. If you think that this is healthy, put a star next to it!

Chapter Eight

Having access to the right resources can be an absolute dealmaker when dealing with grief. In this chapter, we'll delve into a world of helpful resources that can act like a guiding star for families on their journey through grief. Think of these resources as reliable maps that provide support, insights, and a feeling of unity during challenging times.

Super Support

My family and I are blessed with the best family and friends. They held our hands and never let go of it, in addition to offering us legal, financial, and emotional advice. Each aunty and uncle gave us expert advice and supported us in every possible way. They sent us podcasts, books and other resources to help us cope.

Books for Children and Parents

Imagine stepping into a magical library filled with books that understand what you are feeling. Books are like friends who speak to our hearts, and there are some designed to help families during challenging times. For children, some stories share adventures of characters facing loss and change, making them feel less alone. They often use simple language and beautiful illustrations to show emotions, which helps kids navigate their feelings. Some of them are *When Dinosaurs Die* by Laurie Krasny Brown; *The Invisible String* by Patrice Karst; and *The Memory Tree* by Britta Teckentrup. You can read these books to acquire clarity on your thoughts and make sense of your feelings.

Parents, too, have a treasure trove of books offering guidance on how to support their children and themselves through grief. These books provide insights, practical advice, and comforting words, creating a sense of camaraderie with others who have walked similar paths. Sharing these stories becomes a way for families to connect, opening up conversations that might be difficult to start otherwise.

Support Groups and Counseling Services

Support Groups

This was the first time I saw the power of female friendships. My mother's friends became my second mothers. There was a non stop supply of care packages in front of our door. The entire town came together to help. People shared their experiences with us. There was a huge comfort in knowing that we are not alone, that we are loved and protected.

Picture a gathering of superheroes, each with a unique story, ready to share their experiences. Support groups are like these superhero meet-ups, offering families a space to connect, express, and understand. For children, there are groups designed to help them navigate grief through activities, play, and shared experiences. It's a comforting reminder that they're not alone, and others can help them understand the rollercoaster of emotions they are grappling with. Parents can find comfort in adult support groups, where they can share their challenges, exchange coping strategies, and receive empathetic understanding. These groups create a sense of community, where individuals facing similar struggles come together to uplift and empower one another. The shared journey becomes a source of strength, proving that there's power in unity.

<u>*Professional Counseling Services*</u>

Now, think of a wise wizard, someone with the magical ability to guide and heal. Professional counseling services are like these wizards, equipped with the knowledge and skills to support families through grief. For children, specially trained counselors, use creative therapies, play, and conversations to help them express and process their emotions. When I got to the point where I needed an external source of help to aid in understanding my emotions, what I was going through, and how to cope with so many changes in my life, I turned to a therapist. At first, I was skeptical of how much this would really help me. I was nervous because therapy still had an aura of taboo surrounding it, and I was curious to see what would happen in each session and how it would help me. For me, it positively impacted my grieving process. I understood the process better and was able to learn how to connect with my dad even though he was not physically present. It helped me learn how to better communicate my emotions instead of bottling them up, and I was able to find a safe space where I could talk about anything.

In conclusion, these resources for families are like magical tools in a treasure chest. Books, support groups, and professional counseling services offer avenues for healing, understanding, and growth. Families can pick and choose what resonates with them as well as to what extent they want to use them. What you give is what you get—how much effort, willingness, and open-mindedness you practice will determine the degree of positive impacts these tools can have on you.

Chapter Nine

Across the globe, various cultures and communities have created structures and beliefs surrounding grief to aid how their community processes loss, by providing structure to a situation where many feel it is lacked.

I began to understand this concept at a very early age. Ghana, where I grew up, is notorious for its vibrant funerals. I remember seeing colorful posters, billboards, and t-shirts commemorating the deceased. The streets were filled with the beats of drums and people dancing and celebrating the life of a loved one. I always wondered how anyone could find the strength to dance, eat, and enjoy life in such a situation. This paradoxical mix of mourning and celebration seemed incomprehensible to me.

In many other African cultures, death is not seen as an end but as a beginning or a transition. The belief is that ancestors, who have passed on, continue to play an important role in the lives of the living. Funerals, therefore, are not just about mourning a loss but celebrating a life that continues in a different realm.

For example, the Yoruba people of Nigeria view death as a journey to an alternate realm where the deceased can advocate for the living. Their funerals are elaborate, involving rituals that span several days with offerings while the mourners wear traditional attire.

Similarly, the Igbo community in Nigeria sees death as a passage to another dimension where the deceased can mediate on behalf of the living. Funerals are events that can last for weeks, featuring offerings, traditional clothing, and communal singing. The Dogon community in Mali has a unique burial custom where the deceased is buried in a standing position. This practice symbolizes an easier ascension of the soul into the afterlife, aligning with their spiritual beliefs.

In Ghana, the "fantasy coffins" tradition is a unique aspect of funeral customs. Originating in the Greater Accra region, these personalized coffins celebrate the person's life by using their interests, dreams, profession, or social status to commemorate them. Coffin makers have turned death into an art form, creating coffins that honor the individual. Growing up, I marveled at these coffins, which ranged from Coca-Cola bottles and fish to cars, each telling a story about the person and their passions, providing a positive outlook of celebrating the person rather than dwelling on their absence.

As I grappled with grief, I began to use these traditions from the environment around me to shift my perspective. The traditions from various African countries pose the idea of celebrating life, even in the face of death, forming a way to cope with loss. It shifts the focus from the sadness of losing someone to the joy of having known them.

JOURNAL:

Imagine the person who passed away, and what made them unique! What were their passions, what did they love doing, what was their favorite food, did they like any sports? Design a fantasy coffin for them! Once you are done with that, create one for yourself!

Chapter Ten

The Bhagwat Gita, a sacred Hindu scripture, narrates the conversation between Arjuna and Lord Krishna happening on a battlefield. Their discussion occurs just before the Great War, where Arjuna faces a myriad moral dilemmas concerning fighting in the battle against his cousins, friends, teachers, and family members. During this moment, Lord Krishna imparts guidance and wisdom, urging Arjuna to fulfill his duty as a warrior.

Through this scripture, Lord Krishna teaches us that the soul is immortal and that no action can kill the soul. It is only the corporeal body that dies. After death, the soul is reborn into a new body, a new form, but the soul still lives on. Similar to when you put on new clothes, the soul also puts on new bodies. Hindus believe that the body is a temporary container for the immortal soul in this realm. After we die, our physical form deteriorates but our soul continues its journey of birth, death, and rebirth until its final liberation (moksha).

A unique practice in Hinduism is cremation, symbolizing detachment not only from the soul and the body but also from the departed and the living. They believe that the soul of the deceased remains attached to the body after death, and to free it, the body must be cremated to set it free.

Traditionally the eldest male relative is the one who performs the act of cremation. In our case it was my older brother. This moment imposed innumerable emotions, but specifically for me,

I kept on thinking how it was the last time I would ever be near my father's body. This would be the last time I would be able to kiss his cheek, analyze his features, and the last time in my whole life that I will see him.

People who have grown up with different traditions and from various parts of the world may find this tradition strange or obscure, but in reality, it forced me to form a connection with my dad when he passed the physical realm. It urged me to create a spiritual connection and taught me that our relationship was not just limited to seeing him every day but feeling the presence of his soul.

Our final goodbye to my father's physical form lay at the Ganga river, where my family and I stood next to the Ganges. I thought about the millions of individuals who have been in a similar predicament as me, bidding their final farewell to their loved ones. I thought about how many of my ancestors have been here performing the same act, and with that thought my father's final remains, though not without a fight, were taken away by the river.

In The Bhagwat Gita, The Song of God goes like this:

For the soul, there is never birth nor death.
Nor, having once been, does he ever cease to be.
He is unborn, eternal, ever-existing, undying and primeval.
He is not slain when the body is slain.

Buddhism offers similar viewpoints as they believe that there is a continuous cycle of life, death, and rebirth. Their core beliefs include *annica* (impermanence) and that all existence is temporary. They believe in karma, that your actions in this life affect your future existence where good deeds positively affect your rebirth. And *samsara* (rebirth), which is a continuous cycle, gives one a chance to be liberated from this cycle and attain *nirvana* (enlightenment), which is the ultimate goal of a Buddhist.

One unique text in Tibetan Buddhism that further explores the views of death and afterlife is believed to be the Tibetan Book of the Dead or Bardo Thodol. This holy scripture gives clear instructions relating to the intermediate state between life and death called the 'bardo'. The purpose of this practice is to guide the spirit into this state as well as attain a better rebirth or override the state entirely and enter nirvana.

The Tibetan Book of the Dead breaks down bardo into several states. The first one is called Chikhai Bardo where the consciousness is said to experience a phenomenon at the time of death, where get acquainted with the clear light of reality. The second one is the Chonyid Bardo, the state through which a person peruses different visions which are peaceful as well as wrathful. Identifying those visions as images of the person's mind is necessary for advancement. The last of these is the Sidpa Bardo which leads to rebirth. Communicative writing reveals that each of these stages provides chances for spiritual enlightenment and/or salvation, which underlines the roles of awareness and recognition.

One of the features emphasized in the Tibetan Book of the Dead is guidance for the deceased. It gives precise recitations which are to be read to the dying or the dead, to help the consciousness of the former in the bardo realms. The purpose of this guidance is to make the spirits aware of actuality to attain a good rebirth or even illustrate to them the path to enlightenment. What this means is that the locomotive and mangled dead are actively implicated in the ongoing activity of the living through rituals and readings that turn mourning into a work of love.

Epilogue

Grief is a complex and unwanted emotion that most of us feel unlucky to have encountered. It possesses the power to alter lives and people forever and unfortunately, is an emotion every individual will confront at one point in their lives. However, grief does not necessarily need to be overcomplicated or something that you have to grapple with forever. This book aspires to aid readers while they are coming across this emotion and teach them that through processes and mindsets and certain activities, grief too can be eased.

The chapters dedicated to recognizing and understanding grief in children talk about the signs, symptoms, and age-appropriate reactions that may come up. We learned about the different communication strategies to navigate these delicate conversations, emphasizing the importance of age-appropriate language and creating safe spaces for children to express themselves.

Supporting children through grief becomes a focal point, addressing family dynamics, sibling grief, parental grief, and the important role schools and communities play in this journey. We explored creative therapies for children, unveiling the power of art, play, music, and storytelling in helping them express and understand their emotions throughout the grieving process.

Rituals and memorials, highlight the significance of creating meaningful rituals, memorializing loved ones, and celebrating milestones and anniversaries as essential components of the healing process. Building resilience, creating effective and healthy coping skills, developing support systems, and encouraging healthy outlets for grief and tools that empower children to navigate their emotions.

As we conclude this book, a call to action resonates. Grief is a shared experience, and I aim to provide resources and support for families and children walking this path. I am someone who has been deeply affected by grief and writing this book is aimed to prevent confusion and the unnecessary pain that grief caused me. I want people to remember that they are not alone and that this discomfort will ease and it is only temporary. As cliche as it may sound, there is always light at the end of the tunnel!

In closing, I extend my deepest empathy to those grappling with grief. I hope that the insights and tools shared in these chapters serve as a guiding light that offers solace, understanding, and the assurance that, though the journey is challenging, no one has to walk it alone. Let this book be a companion, a resource, and a source of comfort as you navigate the emotion of grief.

Reflections

www.ingramcontent.com/pod-product-compliance
Lightning Source LLC
Chambersburg PA
CBHW020327180726
47991CB00019B/1013